.50

D0564550

We'll pay you to have a checking account.

5¼%

ChekInterest℠

new from

GLENDALE FEDERAL SAVINGS

AND LOAN ASSOCIATION

WITH OVER $4.5 BILLION IN ASSETS AND MORE THAN 90 OFFICES IN CALIFORNIA.

ChekInterest.

A checking account that earns interest daily.

Imagine the convenience of checking and saving in one place, and getting paid to do it. 5¼% annual interest compounded daily. That's our exclusive, new ChekInterest account. What's more, with a qualifying minimum balance, the ChekInterest account is free of the usual bank charges. And insured, risk-free, to $100,000.

First, we make you money. Then, we save you money.

Our ChekInterest program is much more than the usual "negotiable order of withdrawal" account that other financial institutions now offer. For in addition to check writing privileges and high interest, our ChekInterest account offers a myriad of free services, each designed to complement your financial strategy.

You may qualify for a credit card and overdraft protection. Plus free money orders, traveler's cheques, a safe deposit box, and preferred interest rates on various types of loans with certain ChekInterest account packages. Some of these services are offered with minimum savings balances.

Sign up now. Start earning interest at once.

Make a minimum $100 deposit. Your funds will instantly begin earning at the annual interest rate of 5¼%, compounded daily.

nitty gritty books

Cookies	Pressure Cooking	Quiche & Souffle
Cooking for 1 or 2	Food Processor Cookbook	To My Daughter With Love
Chicken Cookbook	Soups & Stews	Natural Foods
Skillet Cookery	Crepes & Omelets	Chinese Vegetarian
Convection Oven	Microwave Cooking	The Jewish Cookbook
Household Hints	Vegetable Cookbook	Working Couples
Seafood Cookbook	Kid's Arts and Crafts	Mexican
Quick Breads	Bread Baking	Sunday Breakfast
Pasta & Rice	The Crockery Pot Cookbook	Fisherman's Wharf Cookbook
Calorie Watchers Cookbook	Classic Greek Cooking	Barbecue Cookbook
Pies & Cakes	Low Carbohydrate Cookbook	Ice Cream Cookbook
Yogurt	Kid's Cookbook	Blender Cookbook
The Ground Beef Cookbook	Italian	The Wok, a Chinese Cookbook
Cocktails & Hors d'Oeuvres	Cheese Guide & Cookbook	Japanese Country
Casseroles & Salads	Miller's German	Fondue Cookbook

designed with giving in mind

Nitty Gritty Productions ● **P.O. Box 5457** ● **Concord, California 94524**

CASSEROLES
Cookbook

by
LOU SEIBERT PAPPAS

Illustrated by Craig Torlucci

A special edition of the
Casseroles & Salads Cookbook

© Copyright 1977
Nitty Gritty Productions
Concord, California

A Nitty Gritty Book*
Published by
Nitty Gritty Productions
P.O. Box 5457
Concord, California 94524

*Nitty Gritty Books - Trademark
Owned by Nitty Gritty Productions
Concord, California

ISBN 0-911954-42-2

Library of Congress Cataloging in Publication Data

Pappas, Lou Seibert
    Casseroles and salads.

    Issued with the author's Salads and casseroles.
Concord, Ca., 1977.
    Includes index.
    1. Casserole cookery.   2. Salads.   1. Title.
TX693.P36   641.8'21   77-22330
ISBN 0-911954-42-2

TABLE OF CONTENTS

INTRODUCTION

A delectable casserole is the busy cook's cherished possession. Generally combining a meat and a vegetable or starch, this meal-in-a-dish can often be made in advance, ready for popping into the oven after a working day or before guests arrive.

The charm of casserole dining depends on a stimulating interplay of ingredients. In this collection of recipes we rely on a variety of international cuisines to bring excitement to peasant-style dishes. We savor the intermingling of pickling spice and cinnamon with beef and onions in a Greek stew; or orange peel and burgundy with lamb and carrots in a French daube; or a Gruyère wine sauce with chicken and veal in a Danish au gratin; or green chiles and Monterey jack cheese with chicken Mexican style. These intriguing compositions of ingredients add a sparkle to everyday fare and company meals.

The casserole dish itself may be any suitable style or shape . . . from a Swiss fondue pot, New England bean pot, French copper ramekin, Moroccan tajine, Spanish paella pan to any other ovenware container. A novel or unexpected casserole can bring enchantment to the presentation of the dish.

With time at a premium for most cooks, it helps to give some preliminary thought to how long the casserole takes to cook, once it is assembled. Thus the casserole recipes are classified according to the time span that they bake. You'll find them grouped in the follow-

1

ing categories: casseroles with a baking time of less than half an hour; those that bake from 30 to 45 minutes; those needing 1 to 1½ hours; those with a 2 hour oven time span; and the long cooking ones requiring 2½ to 4 hours.

Remember the timing of casserole cookery is lengthened considerably if the dish was prepared in advance and refrigerated. The increase will be a minimum of 15 minutes or considerably longer if the ingredients are quite dense.

It is true that reheating mellows and enhances the flavor of many casseroles. The spices,

herbs and other seasoning have a chance to permeate the dish in a subtle, even manner. Some long-simmered meat sauces, such as the Greek Meat Sauce and Bolognese Meat Sauce, are best cooked slowly in quantity in advance. You have the advantage of being able to pull out a container from the refrigerator or freezer on short notice for making a variety of dishes, plus the bonus of added flavor due to double cooking.

Among this collection are casseroles designed for countless dining situations. The Mexican Hamburger Pie or New Joe's Special are ideal last-minute, family dinner entrees. Chicken Saltimbocca or Coq au Vin offer perfect make-ahead dishes for a sit-down guest dinner. The Greek Pitas lend frivolity to a teenage party. For a large buffet for twenty, consider Beef Bourgignonne or Pork a la Kystens. Count on Canneloni or Chile and Cheese Jubilee for appealing brunch entrees. You'll find a wealth of vegetarian and seafood entrees as well.

OVEN TIME
UNDER 30 MINUTES

CHILE PUFF OVEN OMELET

A light, fluffy omelet that holds its puff well after baking.

1/2 cup flour
1 cup milk
1 cup half-and-half
1/4 cup butter
1/2 tsp. salt
dash Tabasco
5 eggs
1 cup (4 ozs.) shredded Monterey jack cheese
1/4 cup diced green chiles

Mix together flour and part of milk in a saucepan. Stir in remaining milk and half-and-half. Heat, stirring, until sauce comes to a boil and thickens. Stir in butter and remove from heat. Beat in salt, Tabasco, eggs and cheese. Add chiles. Turn into a buttered 9 inch square baking pan. Bake in a 400° F. oven 25 to 30 minutes or until puffed and golden brown. Cut into squares. Makes 6 servings.

MUSHROOM RAMEKINS WITH PATÉ

Chilled paté provides a fun fillip to spoon into hot mushroom ramekins for a luncheon entree or as a vegetable accompaniment at dinner.

3 slices firm white bread
6 tbs. butter
1 clove garlic
1 lb. mushrooms, sliced
2 shallots or green onions, chopped
1/2 tsp. salt
1/2 tsp. tarragon
1 tbs. flour
1 cup sour cream
1 cup shredded Gruyère cheese
1 can (2 ozs.) paté with truffles
minced parsley

Cut bread into 1/2 inch cubes. Heat 3 tablespoons butter in a large frying pan. Sauté bread and garlic until golden. Distribute croutons in the bottom of 6 buttered baking dishes, such as small souffle dishes or stoneware pots. Sauté mushrooms in remaining butter just until glazed. Season with salt and tarragon. Blend in flour and cook one minute. Stir in sour cream. Spoon mushrooms into baking dishes. Sprinkle with cheese. Bake in a 400° F. oven 15 minutes or until cheese melts. Spoon a dollop of paté into each dish and sprinkle with parsley. Makes 6 servings.

TURBOT AND SHRIMP CASSEROLE

A restaurant in the seaport of Bergen, Norway, features the day's catch in this vegetable bedecked seafood casserole. It makes an eye-catching party entree.

1 pkg. (8 ozs.) frozen artichoke hearts
2 lbs. turbot or sole fillets
flour, salt and pepper
1/4 cup butter
1/2 lb. mushrooms, sliced

1 tbs. lemon juice
1/3 lb. small cooked shrimp
2 tbs. minced parsley
lemon slices

Cook artichoke hearts as directed and cut in half. Dust fish fillets lightly with flour which has been seasoned with salt and pepper. Melt 2 tablespoons butter in a large frying pan. Saute fillets on both sides until brown. Transfer to a buttered baking dish. Add remaining butter and mushrooms to frying pan. Sprinkle with lemon juice and saute until glazed. Spoon mushrooms over fish. Scatter shrimp and artichoke hearts over mushrooms. Cover dish with foil and bake in a 325° F. oven 15 minutes or until thoroughly heated. Sprinkle with parsley and garnish with lemon. Makes 6 servings.

FILLET OF SOLE FLORENTINE

Fish fillets masked with sour cream bake to tender succulence on a spinach bed.

3 green onions, chopped
2 bunches spinach, chopped
2 tbs. butter
salt and pepper
1-1/3 lbs. sole fillets

garlic salt
6 tbs. sour cream
2 tbs. dry white wine
3 tbs. shredded Parmesan or Romano cheese
paprika

Saute onions and spinach in butter in a large frying pan. Cook just until limp. Transfer with a slotted spoon to a buttered 9 by 9 inch baking dish. Season with salt and pepper to taste. Arrange fish fillets on top of spinach. Sprinkle with salt, pepper and garlic salt. Blend sour cream and wine and spread over fish. Sprinkle with grated cheese and dust with paprika. Bake in a 425° F. oven 15 minutes, or until fish flakes when tested with a fork. Makes 4 servings.

SHRIMP WITH FETA

The waterfront tavernas in Piraeus, Greece, serve this dish in clay ramekins.

1-1/2 lbs. raw medium shrimp
2 tbs. lemon juice
1 medium onion, finely chopped
2 tbs. olive oil
2 cloves garlic, minced
1 can (15 ozs.) tomato puree
1/2 cup *each* dry white wine and clam juice
2 tbs. butter
2 tbs. Pernod or other anise-flavored liqueur
1/2 tsp. dried oregano
3 tbs. chopped parsley
3 cups hot rice pilaff
1/3 lb. feta cheese, cut in 1/2 in. squares

Shell and devein shrimp. Pour lemon juice over shrimp and let stand while preparing

sauce. Saute onions in oil in a large frying pan. Add garlic, tomato puree, wine and clam juice. Simmer uncovered 15 minutes. In another pan saute shrimp in butter until they turn pink. Heat Pernod. Ignite and spoon flaming over shrimp. Add shrimp, oregano and parsley to sauce. Spoon pilaff into one side of 4 buttered, individual ramekins. Add shrimp mixture. Scatter feta over the top pushing it into mixture slightly. Bake in 375° F. oven 15 minutes or until thoroughly heated. Makes 4 servings.

ISTANBUL FISH STEW

The colorful little fish restaurants in the locale where Istanbul fishermen live specialize in this oven-baked white fish stew. Serve with crusty French bread.

2 tbs. olive oil
1 large onion, chopped
1 carrot, peeled and chopped
3 cloves garlic, minced
1 can (6 oz.) tomato paste
3/4 cup dry white wine

1 cup water
salt and pepper to taste
1/2 tsp. crumbled dried basil
2 lbs. turbot or other white fish fillets
chopped parsley

Heat oil in a large Dutch oven or flame-proof casserole. Saute onion and carrot until limp and golden. Add garlic, tomato paste, wine, water, salt, pepper and basil. Cover and simmer 30 minutes or until flavors are blended. Arrange fish fillets in the pan and bake in a 375° F. oven 20 to 30 minutes or until fish flakes when tested with a fork. Sprinkle with parsley. Makes 6 servings.

CHICKEN AND MUSHROOMS SUPREME

Poached chicken is transformed into a party dish by an exquisite cheese sauce and vegetables.

3 lb. broiler-fryer
3 cups chicken broth
3 large carrots, peeled
1 small onion, chopped
5 tbs. butter

2 tbs. flour
1/4 cup heavy cream
1 cup shredded bonbel or Gruyère cheese
3/4 lb. mushrooms
1 can (15 oz.) artichokes *or* hearts of palm

Poach chicken in broth with carrots and onion for 1 hour or until tender. Remove chicken from broth. Let cool slightly. Separate meat from bones. Slice into large pieces. Strain broth and skim fat. Slice cooked carrots diagonally. Melt 3 tablespoons butter. Blend in flour and cook 2 minutes. Stir in 1-1/2 cups broth. Cook, stirring, until thickened. Blend in cream and cheese. Saute mushrooms in remaining butter. Drain artichokes and cut in half, or slice hearts of palm. Layer carrots, chicken, artichokes, and mushrooms in a buttered 1-1/2 quart casserole. Pour sauce over top. Bake in a 375° F. oven 20 minutes or until thoroughly heated. Makes about 6 servings.

CHICKEN SALTIMBOCCA

The Italian "saltimbocca" technique for veal means "jump in the mouth." It also works beautifully with chicken breasts.

8 large split chicken breasts
8 slices prosciutto or choice smoked ham
8 slices (3 to 4 ozs.) Gruyère, Samsoe, or Fontina
1 egg, beaten
1/4 cup fine dry bread crumbs
1 tsp. salt

1/2 tsp. dried tarragon
3 tbs. Romano or Parmesan cheese
3 tbs. butter
1/4 cup chicken broth
1/4 cup dry Vermouth

Bone and skin chicken breasts. Lay each chicken breast out flat. Cover the inner side with a slice *each* of prosciutto and cheese. Roll up and fasten with toothpicks. Dip in egg and then in a mixture of crumbs, salt, tarragon and cheese. Heat butter in large frying pan. Brown rolls. Transfer to a baking dish. Pour broth and wine into frying pan. Bring to a boil and scrape up drippings. Pour over chicken. If desired, refrigerate at this point. Bake in a 350° F. oven, uncovered, until breast meat is white clear to the center, about 20 minutes (or 30 minutes, if refrigerated). Makes 6 to 8 servings.

NEW JOE'S SPECIAL CASSEROLE

This superb baked version of Joe's Special is easily assembled in advance.

2 pkg. (10 ozs. ea.) frozen chopped spinach
1 tbs. butter
1 large onion, chopped
1-1/2 lbs. ground beef
1/2 lb. mushrooms, sliced
1 tsp. salt

1/2 tsp. oregano
1/2 tsp. basil
3/4 cup sour cream
1 egg, lightly beaten
1 cup shredded Gruyère or Samsoe
3/4 cup grated Romano

Thaw spinach and drain well. Press to remove excess moisture. Melt butter in large frying pan. Saute onion until glazed. Add beef and cook until browned. Add mushrooms and cook just until heated. Season with salt, oregano and basil. Remove from heat and stir in spinach. Combine sour cream, egg, Gruyère and half the Romano. Stir into meat mixture. Turn into a buttered 2 quart casserole. Sprinkle with remaining cheese. Bake in 375° F. oven 20 to 25 minutes or until thoroughly heated. Makes 6 servings.

GREEK PITAS

These novel open-faced or pocket sandwiches are a fun choice for teenage gatherings.

1 qt. Greek Meat Sauce, page 86
1/2 cup shredded Romano or Parmesan cheese
1/3 cup pine nuts *or* pistachios, coarsely chopped
6 split and buttered pita breads
2 tomatoes, sliced
4 green onions, chopped
1 avocado, diced

Wrap pita breads in foil. Combine meat sauce, cheese and nuts in a buttered casserole. Bake in a 350° F. oven 15 minutes. Place pita breads in oven with casserole and continue baking 15 to 20 minutes or until both are thoroughly heated. Split breads in half for open face sandwiches, or cut crosswise in half to spoon fillings into the pocket. To serve, arrange breads, meat sauce, and bowls of tomatoes, onions and avocado buffet-style. Let guests assemble their own sandwiches. Makes 6 servings.

TACO CASSEROLE

For a party dinner, accompany this sprightly Mexican-style casserole with sangria, a guacamole salad, hot rolled tortillas and a fresh fruit platter for dessert.

Mexican Meat Sauce
1 pkg. (6 oz.) dip size corn chips
1/2 lb. Monterey jack or Cheddar cheese, shredded
2 cups shredded iceberg lettuce
2 green onions, chopped
3/4 cup sour cream
pitted ripe olives

Prepare meat sauce as directed. Place a layer of corn chips in the bottom of a buttered 2 quart casserole. Sprinkle with 1/3 of the cheese. Cover cheese with half the meat sauce. Add another layer of corn chips, 1/3 of the cheese and remaining meat sauce. Top with remaining corn chips and cheese. (If desired, casserole may be refrigerated at this point.) Bake in a 375° F. oven 20 minutes (40 minutes, if refrigerated), or until hot through. Toss lettuce and onions together. Make a border around the top of casserole. Spoon sour cream in the center.

18

Garnish with olives. Makes 8 to 10 servings.

Mexican Meat Sauce—Finely chop 2 medium onions. Saute in 2 tablespoons butter in a large frying pan until glazed. Add 2 pounds ground beef chuck. Brown until crumbly. Add 1 teaspoon salt, 2 cloves minced garlic, 2 cans (8 oz. *each*) tomato sauce, 2 tablespoons red wine vinegar, 2 teaspoons Mexican seasoning and 1 stick cinnamon. Cover and simmer 15 minutes. Stir in 1 can (1 lb.) dark kidney beans, drained.

MEXICAN HAMBURGER PIE

Green chiles and jack cheese fill a hamburger "crust" for an easily prepared entree.

1 egg
1/4 cup milk
1 slice bread
2 cloves garlic, peeled
1 tbs. parsley sprigs
1/4 medium onion
1/2 tsp. salt
1 lb. ground beef chuck
1/3 cup chili sauce
1 cup (4 ozs.) Monterey jack cheese, shredded
2 tbs. diced green chiles
2 tbs. minced sweet onion
1/2 tsp. Mexican seasoning

Place egg, milk, bread, garlic, parsley, onion and salt in a blender container and puree.

Crumble meat into a mixing bowl. Add blended mixture and mix together well. Pat meat into a buttered 9-inch pie pan covering the bottom and sides in an even layer. Spread chili sauce over the center of the meat. Sprinkle with cheese, diced chiles, onions and Mexican seasoning. Bake in a 425° F. oven 15 to 20 minutes, or until meat is no longer pink and cheese is melted. Cut into wedges. Makes 4 servings.

Italian Hamburger Pie—Prepare meat mixture and pat into a 9-inch pie pan as directed. For the topping, substitute 1/3 cup catsup for chili sauce and Cheddar cheese for jack cheese. Saute 1/4 pound mushrooms and 2 tablespoons chopped onion in 1 tablespoon butter until limp. Spread evenly over cheese. Sprinkle with 1/2 teaspoon dried basil and 2 tablespoons grated Parmesan cheese. Bake as directed.

STACKED TACO WEDGES

Tortillas layered with spicy meat sauce and chile-spiced cheese bake into a savory pie that cuts into ribboned wedges.

1 tsp. Mexican seasoning
2 cups Greek Meat Sauce, page 86
2 cups grated Monterey jack cheese
1 cup (1/2 pt.) sour cream
2 tbs. chopped green chiles

3 green onions, chopped
butter
6 flour tortillas
1 avocado

Stir Mexican seasoning into meat sauce until well blended. Combine cheese, 1/2 cup sour cream, chiles and onions. Lightly butter tortillas. Place 1 tortilla in a 9-inch pie pan. Cover with 1/3 of the meat sauce. Top with another tortilla. Spread with 1/3 of the cheese mixture. Repeat alternating layers with the 4 remaining tortillas. Bake in 350° F. oven 20 minutes-or until thoroughly heated. Slice avocado. Top casserole with the remaining sour cream. Place avocado slices in a pinwheel on top. Cut into wedges to serve. Makes 4 to 6 servings.

ENCHILADAS PICADILLO

1 tbs. olive oil
2 medium onions, chopped
2 lbs. ground beef chuck
2 sticks cinnamon
10 whole cloves
1-1/2 tsp. salt
1 can (6 ozs.) tomato paste
1/3 cup red wine vinegar

4 cloves garlic, minced
1 can (1 lb.) refried beans
1 can (16 ozs.) tomato sauce
2 tsp. Mexican seasoning
12 flour tortillas
1-1/2 cups shredded Cheddar cheese
sour cream
ripe pitted olives

Heat oil in large frying pan. Saute onions until limp. Add meat and brown lightly. Tie cinnamon sticks and cloves in a piece of cheesecloth. Add to meat along with salt, tomato paste, vinegar and garlic. Cover and simmer 30 minutes. Remove spices and stir in beans. Combine tomato sauce and seasoning. Bring to a boil. Pour half into a 9 by 13 inch baking pan. Spoon a ribbon of filling down the center of each tortilla and roll up. Place in baking pan. Pour remaining tomato sauce over rolls and sprinkle with cheese. Bake uncovered in a 350° F. oven 20 minutes. Serve with sour cream and olives. Makes 6 to 8 servings.

CANNELLONI

This renowned Italian dish freezes well, ready for unexpected guests.

2 onions, chopped
1/4 butter
1 lb. *each* ground beef and veal*
3 cloves garlic, minced
1 pt. ricotta cheese
2 cups grated Romano or Parmesan cheese
5 egg yolks
1-1/2 tsp. salt
1 pkg. (9 ozs.) frozen chopped spinach, thawed and drained
1/4 tsp. nutmeg
1 lb. cannelloni noodles *or* 4 dozen 6-inch crepes
Bechamel Sauce, page 25

Saute onions in butter until golden. Add meats and garlic. Cook until browned. Combine ricotta, 1 cup Romano cheese, egg yolks, salt, spinach and nutmeg. Stir into meat mixture. Cut cannelloni into 4 or 5 inch lengths. Cook in boiling salted water until al dente. Lay flat on paper toweling to drain. To assemble, place about 3 tablespoons filling in a ribbon down one side of each pasta. Roll up to enclose. Pour a thin layer of Bechamel Sauce in a shallow ovenproof baking dish. Place canneloni seam side down in pan. Repeat until all are filled. Cover with remaining sauce. Sprinkle remaining Romano cheese over top. Bake in 425° F. oven 10 to 12 minutes or until thoroughly heated. Makes about 4 dozen canneloni.

Bechamel Sauce—Melt 3/4 cup butter. Blend in 3/4 cup flour. Cook, stirring, 2 minutes. Gradually stir in 1 quart milk and 1 cup rich chicken stock. Cook, stirring, until thickened. Season with 2 teaspoons salt and 1/2 teaspoon *each* nutmeg and pepper. Blend in 1 cup grated Romano cheese.

*Substitute ground turkey for ground beef, if desired.

TURKISH KÖFTE CASSEROLE WITH YOGURT

From Sofra, a charming triple-storied businessmen's restaurant in Istanbul, come these highly-spiced meatballs bathed in tomato gravy and cooled with yogurt. Hot pita bread is a proper accompaniment.

Tomato Onion Sauce, page 27
1-1/2 lbs. ground beef
1 lb. ground veal *or* lamb
2 slices fresh bread
1/3 cup water
3 eggs
2 tsp. salt

4 cloves garlic, minced
1/2 tsp. ground cumin
1/4 tsp. ground pepper
2 tbs. chopped parsley
2 tbs. butter
yogurt
chopped parsley

Prepare sauce as directed. Combine ground meats in a mixing bowl. Place bread, water, eggs, salt, garlic, cumin and pepper in a blender container. Puree until blended. Pour puree over meat. Add parsley and mix until blended. Shape into 1-1/4 inch balls. Melt butter in large frying pan. Brown meatballs on all sides. Transfer to a baking dish. Pour Tomato Onion Sauce over meatballs. Bake in a 350° F. oven 20 minutes, or until thoroughly

heated. Garnish each serving with a generous dollop of yogurt and a sprinkling of parsley. Makes about 8 servings.

Tomato Onion Sauce—Peel and finely chop 1 small onion. Saute in 1 tablespoon butter until golden. Add 1-1/2 cups beef broth, 3 tablespoons tomato paste and 3 tablespoons dry red wine. Simmer 15 minutes, stirring occasionally.

27

OVEN TIME
30 TO 45 MINUTES

SMOTHERED FISH PLAKA STYLE

Fish steaks are sandwiched between a melange of vegetables in this oven entree.

1/3 cup olive oil
1 medium onion, chopped
2 stalks celery, finely chopped
3 small carrots, finely sliced
1 bunch green onions, chopped
1 bunch spinach, chopped
1/2 cup chopped parsley

1 can (6 oz.) tomato sauce
3 cloves garlic, minced
salt and freshly ground pepper
2-1/2 lbs. sea bass, halibut *or*
    other firm white fish steaks
lemon wedges

Heat oil in a large frying pan. Saute onion, celery, carrots and green onions until glazed. Add spinach, parsley, tomato sauce, garlic, salt and pepper to taste. Cover and simmer 15 minutes. Spoon half the vegetable mixture into a buttered baking pan. Cover with fish steaks. Spoon remaining vegetable mixture on top. Cover and bake in a 350° F. oven 45 minutes, or until fish flakes when tested with a fork. Serve with lemon wedges. Makes 8 servings.

BASQUE CHICKEN AND SAUSAGE

This elegant chicken stew welcomes a variety of vegetables. Serve it in individ᾽ ᾽l ramekins with garlic buttered crusty rolls.

1 carrot, peeled and chopped
1 medium onion, peeled and chopped
1 tbs. *each* butter and olive oil
3 lb. broiler-fryer, cut-up *or*
   4 *each* chicken legs and thighs
6 mild Italian sausages
1 tsp. salt
1/2 tsp. crumbled dried tarragon

2 cloves garlic, minced
1/3 cup dry white wine
1/3 cup chicken broth
1 pkg. (9 or 10 ozs.) frozen artichoke hearts
   or baby lima beans, thawed, *or*
   6 crookneck squash, sliced lengthwise
1 cup cherry tomatoes, halved
2 tbs. minced parsley

Using a Dutch oven or flameproof casserole, saute carrot and onion in butter and oil until glazed. Push to the sides of the pan and add chicken pieces. Brown chicken on all sides. Add sausages, salt, tarragon, garlic, wine, broth and vegetable. Cover and bake in a 350° F. oven 30 to 35 minutes, or until tender. Scatter cherry tomatoes and parsley over the top just before serving. Makes 6 servings.

31

MEXICAN CHICKEN AND CHILE CASSEROLE

This Latin-inspired casserole lends itself to day-ahead preparation.

2 3-lb. broiler-fryer chickens
1 qt. chicken broth
2 tbs. cornstarch mixed with 2 tbs. cold water
1 medium onion, finely chopped
1 green pepper, chopped
1 tbs. olive oil
1 can (4 oz.) diced green chiles
2 cloves garlic, minced

1 tsp. Mexican seasoning
1/2 lb. (2 cups) shredded
   Monterey jack cheese
1/2 cup shredded Parmesan cheese
1 cup sour cream
1 cup cherry tomatoes, halved (optional)
cilantro sprigs for garnish

Wash chickens. Bring broth to boil in a large soup kettle. Add chickens. Cover, and simmer 1 hour or until drumsticks move easily. Lift chickens from broth and let cool. Remove meat and discard bones and skin. Cut meat into large strips. Strain and chill broth then lift off fat. Cook broth uncovered over high heat until reduced to 1 cup. Stir cornstarch paste into reduced broth. Cook, stirring, until very thick. Set aside. Saute onion and pepper in oil until limp. Add to thickened sauce along with chiles, garlic and Mexican seasoning.

Place half of chicken in a 7 by 11 inch baking dish. Add half the chile sauce. Sprinkle with half the cheeses. Add remaining chicken and cover with sauce. Spread sour cream over top. Sprinkle with remaining cheeses. (If desired, cover casserole and chill at this point.) Bake uncovered in a 325° F. oven 45 minutes (1 hour if refrigerated) or until thoroughly heated. Garnish with cilantro sprigs and cherry tomatoes. Makes 8 servings.

DANISH CHICKEN AND VEAL AU GRAUTIN

This specialty from the Coq 'd Or in Copenhagen shows off a trio of meats in a wine-scented cheese sauce. A golden piping of mashed potatoes often rims the dish.

1 lb. ground veal
3 tbs. flour
1 egg
1/2 tsp. salt
1/8 tsp. nutmeg
1 green onion, chopped (white part only)
1/3 cup milk
1/4 cup butter
1-1/2 lbs. chicken breasts, boned and skinned
1/2 lb. cooked ham, cut in julienne strips
Wine Cheese Sauce, page 35

Mix veal, flour, egg, salt, nutmeg, onion and milk together. Heat 2 tablespoons butter in a large frying pan. Drop rounded teaspoons of the meat mixture into pan. Saute until browned on all sides. Remove and set aside. Add 2 more tablespoons butter to pan. Saute chicken until it turns white. Combine meat balls, chicken, ham and Wine Cheese Sauce. Turn into a greased baking dish. Bake in a 375° F. oven 30 minutes or until thoroughly heated. Makes 8 to 10 servings.

Wine Cheese Sauce—Melt 3 tablespoons butter in a saucepan. Blend in 3 tablespoons flour and 1 teaspoon Dijon-style mustard. Cook, stirring, 2 minutes. Add 3/4 cup chicken stock, 1/2 cup half-and-half and 1/4 cup dry white wine. Cook, stirring, until thickened. Gradually add 1 cup shredded Gruyère or Samsoe cheese. Stir until melted. Remove from heat and add 1 jar (2 oz.) sliced pimientoes, drained. If desired, add 1/2 pound sauteed sliced mushrooms.

PASTITSIO

Serve this popular Greek dish with roast chicken or ham, or by itself.

1 pkg. (14 oz.) large elbow macaroni
1/4 cup butter
1/4 cup flour
3 cups milk
1/2 tsp. salt
1/8 tsp. nutmeg

1/8 tsp. freshly ground pepper
5 eggs
1 qt. Greek Meat Sauce, page 86
1-1/2 cups (6 ozs.) grated Romano
cinnamon

Cook macaroni in a large amount of boiling salted water until barely tender, about 12 minutes. Drain and rinse under cold water. Drain again. Melt butter in saucepan. Blend in flour. Remove from heat and gradually stir in milk. Cook, stirring constantly, until slightly thickened. Season with salt, nutmeg and pepper. Beat eggs until light. Quickly stir hot sauce into beaten eggs. Butter a 9 by 13 inch baking pan. Alternate layers of macaroni, meat sauce and cheese. Dust lightly with cinnamon. Pour custard sauce over top. Finish with a little more cheese. Bake in a 350° F. oven 40 minutes, or until custard is set and top is browned. Let cool slightly, then cut into squares. Makes 15 servings.

ZUCCHINI MOUSSAKA

In this version of Moussaka a golden brown custard topping covers layers of meat sauce and sauteed squash or other vegetables.

2 lbs. zucchini
1/3 cup olive oil
1/4 cup *each* butter and flour
3 cups milk
3/4 tsp. salt
1/8 tsp. nutmeg
5 eggs
1 qt. Greek Meat Sauce, page 86
1/4 cup fine dry bread crumbs
3/4 cup grated Romano or Parmesan cheese

Trim ends from squash. Slice lengthwise or on the diagonal about 1/4 inch thick. Saute in oil, until crisp tender. Turn frequently. Melt butter in saucepan. Blend in flour. Gradually stir in milk. Cook, stirring constantly, until thickened. Add salt and nutmeg. Beat eggs until light. Blend hot sauce into the eggs. Arrange a layer of squash in a buttered 9 by 13 inch baking pan. Cover bottom of pan with half the meat sauce, add half of crumbs and half the cheese. Cover with another layer of squash, remaining meat sauce and crumbs. Spoon custard over the top and sprinkle with remaining cheese. Bake in a 350° F. oven 45 minutes, or until set and lightly browned. Let stand 10 minutes before cutting into squares. Makes 12 to 15 servings.

Eggplant Moussaka—Instead of the squash, substitute 2 large eggplants, sliced 3/4 inch thick. Place slices on 2 oiled 10 by 15-inch baking sheets. Bake in a 400° F. oven 30 minutes, or until tender, turning once.

Mushroom and Artichoke Moussaka—Instead of the squash and oil, substitute 1 pound mushrooms, sliced and sauteed in 3 tablespoons butter and 2 packages (8 oz. *each*) frozen artichoke hearts, cooked in boiling salted water until tender, about 7 minutes.

LASAGNE

Double this favorite make-ahead recipe . . . one for the party; one for the freezer.

Italian Sausage Meat Sauce
12 ozs. lasagne noodles
boiling salted water

1 lb. ricotta cheese
1 lb. mozzarella cheese
1/2 cup Romano or Parmesan cheese

Prepare meat sauce. Cook noodles in boiling salted water until barely tender. Drain and rinse under cold water. Drain well again. Arrange about 1/3 of the noodles in a greased 9 by 13-inch baking pan. Spread 1/3 of meat sauce over noodles. Top with 1/3 *each* of the ricotta and mozzarella. Repeat layers two more times. Sprinkle with Romano. Bake uncovered in 350° F. oven 30 to 40 minutes or until browned. Makes 8 servings.

Italian Sausage Meat Sauce—Heat 1-1/2 tablespoons *each* butter and oil in frying pan. Saute 1 chopped onion, 1 grated carrot and 1 chopped celery stalk. Add 1 pound beef and 1/2 pound crumbled Italian sausage. Cook until browned. Stir in 1 teaspoon *each* salt and dried basil, 1 can (15 ozs.) tomato puree, 3 tablespoons tomato paste, 3 cloves garlic, minced and 1/4 cup dry red wine. Cover and simmer 1-1/2 hours.

BEEF AND SQUASH STRATA

Italian Meat Sauce
1 lb. zucchini
1 tbs. butter
garlic salt
2 medium tomatoes, thinly sliced

1 pt. small curd cottage cheese
2 eggs
1/2 cup grated Parmesan or Romano
1/2 cup shredded Gruyère or Samsoe
2 green onions, chopped

Prepare meat sauce as directed. Trim ends from zucchini and thinly slice on the diagonal. Stir-fry in butter 2 to 3 minutes, or until crisp tender. Place in a buttered 10 inch round baking dish. Sprinkle lightly with garlic salt. Spoon meat sauce over zucchini. Cover with a layer of tomatoes. Beat cottage cheese and eggs together. Stir in Parmesan, Gruyère and onions. Pour over tomatoes. Bake in a 375° F. oven 35 minutes, or until set and lightly browned. Cut into wedges. Makes 6 servings.

Italian Meat Sauce—Chop 1 medium onion. Saute in 1 tablespoon olive oil until limp. Add 1-1/2 pounds ground beef chuck and cook until browned. Stir in 1 teaspoon salt, 1/2 teaspoon *each* dried basil and marjoram, 1 can (8 oz.) tomato sauce and 1/4 cup dry red wine. Cover and simmer 45 minutes. Use as directed.

SQUASH-SEASON OVEN FRITTATA

Green and gold garden squash, ham strips and freshly shredded Romano enliven this frittata which cuts into wedges for easy serving.

2 zucchini	1/4 tsp. salt
2 yellow crookneck squash	1/4 tsp. freshly ground pepper
3 tbs. olive oil	1/4 cup chopped parsley
3 green onions, chopped	1/3 cup julienne ham strips
1 clove garlic, minced	6 eggs, lightly beaten
1/4 tsp. basil	1/2 cup grated Parmesan cheese

Slice squash thinly. Sprinkle with salt and let stand 10 minutes. Rinse under cold water. Drain and pat out excess moisture with paper towels. Heat oil in a large frying pan. Saute squash, onions and garlic with basil, salt and pepper until limp. Turn into a buttered 9 inch round baking dish. Scatter parsley and ham over squash. Pour eggs over top and sprinkle with cheese. Bake in a 350° F. oven 35 minutes or until set. Makes 6 servings.

CHILE AND CHEESE JUBILEE

This casserole is ideal for a Mexican brunch. Serve with grilled pork sausages, guacamole salad, fresh pineapple and sangria.

6 eggs
1 cup light cream
1-1/2 tsp. baking powder
1/2 tsp. salt
2 tbs. flour
1 can (14 oz.) diced green chiles
1 lb. Cheddar cheese, grated
1 lb. Monterey jack cheese, grated
1 tbs. butter

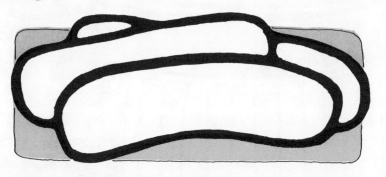

Beat eggs until light. Stir in cream, baking powder, salt and flour. Lightly butter a 2-quart casserole. Sprinkle half the chiles in casserole. Cover with half the cheese. Repeat with remaining chiles and cheese. Pour egg mixture over top. Dot with butter. Bake in a 350° F. oven 40 to 45 minutes, or until puffed and set. Makes 8 servings.

OVEN TIME
1 TO 1-1/2 HOURS

COQ AU VIN

This classic French chicken dish, reminiscent of one sampled in Nice, has lovely rich wine juices that call for buttered rice on the side.

3 tbs. butter
4 *each* chicken legs, thighs and breasts
3/4 lb. small boiling onions
1 tbs. brown sugar
1-1/2 cups dry red wine
3/4 cup chicken stock
salt and pepper
1 clove garlic, minced
1/8 tsp. *each* nutmeg and marjoram
1 tbs. cornstarch
1 tbs. cold water
1/3 lb. mushrooms

Heat 1 tablespoon butter in a large frying pan. Brown chicken well on all sides.

46

Transfer to a casserole. Peel onions and cut a cross in the root end of each. Add to frying pan with 1 tablespoon butter. Shake pan until onions are glazed. Add sugar and cook until caramelized. Spoon over chicken. Pour the wine and stock into frying pan. Bring to a boil, scraping up drippings. Pour over chicken. Season with salt, pepper, garlic, nutmeg and marjoram. Cover and bake in a 350° F. oven 1 hour, or until chicken is barely tender. Mix cornstarch and water in a small saucepan. Drain juices from casserole into saucepan with cornstarch. Cook, stirring, until thickened. Pour over chicken. Saute whole trimmed mushrooms in remaining butter. Add to chicken and continue to bake until thoroughly heated about 15 minutes longer. Makes 6 to 8 servings.

VEAL AND WATER CHESTNUT CASSEROLE

The delightful crunch of water chestnuts enlivens this savory party stew. Serve in individual ramekins with pilaff alongside.

2 lbs. boneless veal
4 tbs. butter
1 onion, chopped
3 cloves garlic, minced
1 tsp. salt
freshly ground pepper
1 cup beef or chicken stock

1 tsp. grated lemon peel
1/8 tsp. ground nutmeg
1 lb. mushrooms, sliced or quartered
1 can (6 oz.) water chestnuts
1 cup heavy cream
3 tbs. brandy or cognac
finely chopped parsley

Cut veal into 1-1/4 inch pieces. Brown in 2 tablespoons of butter in a Dutch oven or flame-proof casserole. Add onion and cook until limp. Stir in garlic, salt, pepper, stock, lemon peel and nutmeg. Cover and bake in a 325° F. oven 1 hour. Saute mushrooms in remaining butter. Thinly slice chestnuts. Add to meat along with mushrooms, cream and brandy. Bake uncovered 30 minutes longer, or until meat is tender. Sprinkle with parsley. Makes 6 servings.

CRETAN STYLE VEAL

A canopied outdoor taverna at the charming Cretan resort of Aghios Nikolai offers this tantalizing stew in fat clay pots.

2 lbs. boneless stewing veal
2 tbs. butter
1 large onion, finely chopped
6 small potatoes
6 whole cloves
4 cloves garlic, minced
2 tsp. salt

1/4 tsp. freshly ground pepper
2 cups water
3 tbs. tomato paste
1/4 cup white wine vinegar
1 stick cinnamon
1/2 cup grated Romano cheese

Cut veal into 1-1/2 inch cubes. Melt butter in a large Dutch oven or flame-proof casserole. Brown meat in butter. Add onion and cook until glazed. Peel potatoes and cut in lengthwise strips. Tie whole cloves in a small piece of cheesecloth or place in a tea ball. Add to meat along with garlic, salt, pepper, water, tomato paste, vinegar, cinnamon and potatoes. Stir to blend and bring to a boil. Cover and bake in a 325° F. oven 1-1/2 hours or until meat is fork tender. Remove spices. Sprinkle with cheese. Makes 6 servings.

VEAL PAPRIKA

This sour cream-encriched stew is from an Austrian wine house in Grinzing. Accompany with hot noodles, pickled beets and coleslaw, and finish with an almond torte!

2 lbs. boneless stewing veal or calf
3 tbs. butter
1 large onion, finely chopped
2 cloves garlic, minced
2 tsp. paprika
1-1/2 tsp. salt
freshly ground pepper
1 tsp. caraway seed

1 tomato, peeled and chopped
1/2 cup dry white wine
1/2 cup chicken stock
1/2 lb. small mushrooms
1 tbs. cornstarch
1 tbs. cold water
1/2 cup sour cream
chopped parsley

Cut veal into 1-1/4 inch cubes. Melt 1 tablespoon butter in a large Dutch oven. Saute onion until glazed. Push to the sides of pan. Add meat and brown on all sides. Stir in garlic and paprika until well blended. Add salt, pepper, caraway, tomato, wine and stock. Cover and bake in a 325° F. oven 1 to 1-1/2 hours, or until meat is tender. Remove from oven. Saute mushrooms in remaining butter. Add to meat. Place Dutch oven over direct heat. Bring the

juices to a boil. Combine cornstarch and water. Stir into juices. Cook, stirring, until thickened. Blend in sour cream and heat to serving temperature. Sprinkle with parsley. Makes 6 servings.

VEAL AND ARTICHOKE MARENGO

Baby beef or calf substitutes nicely for veal in this Italian stew.

2 lbs. stewing veal
2 tbs. butter or olive oil
1 large onion, chopped
2 large tomatoes
3 cloves garlic, minced
1 cup dry vermouth
1 cup chicken or beef stock

2 tsp. salt
1/2 tsp. dried basil
freshly ground pepper
2 pkg. (9 oz. each) frozen artichoke hearts, thawed
1 tbs. white wine vinegar
3 tbs. chopped parsley

Cut veal into 1-1/4 inch pieces. Heat butter in a Dutch oven or flame-proof casserole. Brown meat on all sides. Add onion and cook until glazed. Peel and chop 1 tomato. Add to meat along with garlic, vermouth, chicken stock, salt, basil and pepper. Cover and bake in a 325° F. oven 1 hour or until meat is almost tender. Add artichoke hearts and vinegar. Cook 15 minutes longer. Sprinkle with parsley. Makes 6 servings.

Note: If desired thicken pan juices with 2 tablespoons cornstarch blended with 2 tablespoons cold water.

YAYA'S OVEN GARDEN STEW

In the Greek tongue, Yaya means Grandmother, and this is her way of turning summer's garden bounty into a heavenly melange.

1 medium onion, chopped
3 tbs. olive oil
3 medium potatoes
1/2 lb. green beans
4 small zucchini
4 small crookneck squash
3 leaves mint, chopped

2 cloves garlic, minced
1 tomato, chopped
2 tbs. chopped parsley
salt and pepper
1 cup Greek Meat Sauce (optional), page 86
grated Romano cheese

Saute onion in 1 tablespoon oil in a frying pan until golden. Peel and slice potatoes. Cut beans in 2 inch pieces. Slice squash. In a 9 by 13 inch baking dish, alternate layers of potatoes, onion, squash and green beans. Scatter mint, garlic, tomato and parsley over top. Drizzle with remaining oil. Season with salt and pepper. If desired, add Greek Meat Sauce. Bake in a 375° F. oven 1 hour, or until vegetables are tender. Pass cheese to spoon over stew. Makes 6 to 8 servings.

BAKED KRAUT AND BEEF DINNER

This midwestern entree has an Eastern European heritage. It's a homely but good, fast-to-assemble casserole meal.

1 medium onion, chopped
1 tbs. butter or oil
1 lb. lean ground beef
1 tsp. salt
2 cloves garlic, minced
freshly ground pepper

1/3 cup uncooked long grain white rice
1/2 cup tomato sauce
1 can (1 lb.) sauerkraut, drained
1 cup rich chicken or beef stock
sour cream or yogurt

Saute onion in butter until golden. Push to the sides of the pan. Add meat and cook until browned. Stir in salt, garlic, pepper, rice and tomato sauce. Butter a 9 inch square baking dish. Spread half the sauerkraut in bottom of dish. Top with meat mixture. Cover meat with remaining sauerkraut. Pour stock over top. Cover with foil. Bake in 350° F. oven 1-1/2 hours. Cut in squares and serve topped with a spoonful of sour cream or yogurt. Makes 6 servings.

55

IRISH STEW

For a Shamrock's Day buffet feature this hearty stew.

2-1/2 lbs. boneless lamb shoulder
1/4 cup flour
2 tsp. salt
1 tsp. dry mustard
2 tbs. bacon drippings or butter
1 medium onion, chopped
8 small whole onions, peeled
2 carrots, peeled and sliced diagonally
2 turnips, peeled and cut in wedges
1/2 tsp. thyme
2 cups water
1 pkg. (9 oz.) petit peas, thawed
2 tbs. *each* sugar and vinegar

Cut lamb into cubes. Dredge in flour seasoned with salt and mustard. Heat bacon

drippings in large frying pan. Brown meat and chopped onion. Transfer to a casserole. Saute small whole onions in frying pan until glazed. Add to casserole along with carrots, turnips, thyme and water. Cover and bake in a 350° F. oven 1-1/2 hours, or until meat and vegetables are tender. Stir in peas, sugar and vinegar. Bake 5 to 10 minutes longer. Makes 8 servings.

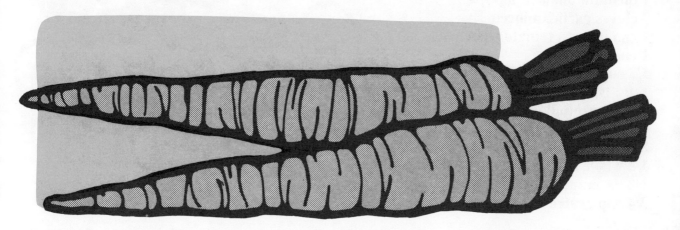

PASTITSADO

This specialty of Corfu, an Ionian island on the NW coast of Greece, pairs spiced beef with a tear-shaped pasta called manestra, and Romano cheese.

1 tbs. olive oil
2 lbs. cubed stewing beef or veal
1 medium onion, chopped
3 cloves garlic, minced
1 can (6 ozs.) tomato paste
1 cup water
1/2 cup dry white wine
1-1/2 tsp. salt
freshly ground pepper
1/2 stick cinnamon
8 whole cloves
1/2 whole allspice
1/2 lb. manestra or elbow macaroni
3/4 cup grated Romano cheese

58

Heat oil in large frying pan. Brown meat on all sides. Add onion and garlic. Saute until glazed. Transfer to a casserole with a tight fitting cover. Add tomato paste, water, wine, salt and pepper to pan drippings. Stir over medium heat until mixture boils. Tie cinnamon stick,

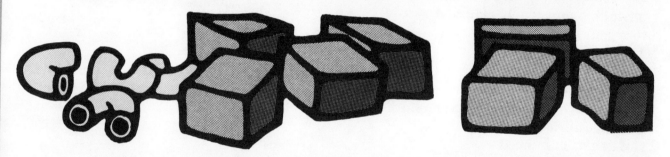

cloves and allspice in a small piece of cheesecloth. Add to casserole. Cover and bake in a 350° F. oven 1-1/2 hours, or until meat is almost tender. Cook pasta in boiling salted water until "al dente". Drain well. Combine with meat and sauce. Continue baking 15 to 20 minutes longer. At serving time, stir in cheese and serve in shallow soup plates. Makes 6 servings.

OVEN BEEF STROGANOFF

Serve this tantalizing stew with noodles or potato dumplings to absorb the juices.

1 tbs. *each* butter and oil
2 lbs. round steak, cut in strips
1 medium onion, finely chopped
3 tbs. flour
1/4 cup tomato paste
1 can (10-1/2 oz.) consomme
1/2 cup dry red wine
1-1/2 tsp. *each* salt and Worcestershire sauce
dash angostura bitters
2 cloves garlic, minced
1 lb. mushrooms, sliced
3 tbs. butter
1/2 cup sour cream

Heat butter and oil in a large frying pan. Brown meat well. Transfer to a casserole with

OVEN TIME
2 HOURS

CASSEROLE PATÉ WITH PINE NUTS

Serve this cool veal paté ribboned with ham and flecked with pine nuts for a party first course or a summer supper.

2 large onions, finely chopped
1/4 cup butter
3 cloves garlic, minced
1/2 tsp. thyme
1/2 tsp. ground allspice
1/4 tsp. nutmeg
1/4 tsp. ground cloves
1/4 cup pale dry sherry
1-1/2 lbs. ground veal
1 lb. ground pork

3 eggs
1/3 cup heavy cream
1/4 cup flour
2 tbs. brandy or cognac
1-1/2 tsp. salt
freshly ground pepper
3 slices bacon
1/4 lb. smoked sliced ham
1 pkg. (2 oz.) pine nuts

Using a large frying pan saute onions in butter until golden. Add garlic, thyme, allspice, nutmeg, cloves and sherry. Cook down until juices have evaporated. Cool. Place veal, pork, eggs, cream, flour, brandy, salt, pepper and onion mixture in a large bowl. Mix until blended. Line a 2 quart terrine, casserole, or 9 by 5 inch loaf pan with bacon. Cover bacon with 1/3 of the meat mixture. Top meat layer with half the ham and 1/3 of the pine nuts. Add another 1/3 of the meat, remaining ham and another 1/3 of the nuts. Make a final layer with remaining meat. Top with remaining nuts. Cover pan with foil and place in a shallow pan containing 1 inch hot water. Bake in a 325° F. oven 2 hours. Uncover and bake 20 minutes longer. Cool slightly then refrigerate until well chilled. Serve sliced from the casserole, accompanied by French bread and sweet butter. Makes 10 to 12 servings.

FLEMISH BEEF STEW

Beer lends a spicy tang to this robust stew that welcomes pilaff or noodles alongside.

2 lbs. boneless beef chuck
4 medium onions
1/4 cup *each* butter and flour
1-1/2 tsp. salt
1/4 tsp. pepper
2 cloves garlic, minced

1 bay leaf
1/2 tsp. thyme
2 tbs. chopped parsley
1 tbs. cider vinegar
1 tbs. brown sugar
1 bottle (12 ozs.) dark beer

Cut chuck into 1-1/4 inch pieces. Thinly slice onions. Melt half of the butter in a large frying pan. Saute onions until limp and golden brown. Transfer to a casserole with a tight fitting cover. Combine flour, salt and pepper in a paper bag. Add meat and shake until coated. Add remaining butter to frying pan. Brown meat on all sides. Transfer to casserole. Add garlic, bay leaf, thyme, parsley, vinegar, brown sugar and beer. Cover and bake in 325° F. oven 2 hours or until meat is fork tender. Makes about 6 servings.

OSSO BUCO

The Milanese receive credit for this renowned style of braising veal shanks. Crusty French bread and risotto are choice companions for absorbing the flavorful wine sauce.

6 (2 in. thick) veal shanks
flour
1-1/2 tbs. butter
1-1/2 tbs. olive oil
salt and freshly ground pepper
1 medium onion, finely chopped
1 small carrot, peeled and grated

1 cup dry white wine or Vermouth
1 tsp. chicken stock base
1/3 cup tomato sauce
1 clove garlic, minced
1-1/2 grated lemon peel
2 tbs. minced parsley
1 lemon, thinly sliced

Roll veal shanks in flour. Shake off excess. Heat butter and oil in a large frying pan. Brown shanks well on all sides. Sprinkle with salt and pepper. Transfer to a casserole. Add onion and carrot to frying pan and saute until limp. Add wine, stock base, tomato sauce and garlic. Bring to a boil and pour over shanks. Cover and bake in a 350° F. oven 2 hours, or until meat is tender. Mix lemon peel and parsley together. Sprinkle over the meat. Garnish with lemon slices. Makes 6 servings.

LAMB SHANKS EN DAUBE

The zest of orange peel permeates this country dish from Provence.

2 tbs. olive oil
1 large onion, chopped
1 carrot, peeled and chopped
4 (about 3 lbs.) lamb shanks
1 cup beef or chicken stock
3/4 cup dry red wine

1 tsp. salt
1/2 tsp. thyme
2 cloves garlic, minced
3 strips orange peel
1 cup cherry tomatoes, halved
2 tbs. chopped parsley

Heat oil in a Dutch oven or flame-proof casserole. Saute onion and carrot until limp. Push to the sides of the pan. Add shanks and brown on all sides. Stir in stock, wine, salt, thyme, garlic and orange peel. Cover and cook in a 325° F. oven 2 hours or until shanks are tender. Remove to a platter and keep warm. Over direct heat, boil down pan juices until reduced slightly. Skim fat. Add tomatoes and spoon sauce over shanks. Sprinkle with parsley. Makes 4 servings.

PORK A LA KYSTENS

An Inn on the Danish seaside features this easy, exotic party dish. It is ideal for a make-ahead buffet.

2 lbs. boneless pork loin
peel of 1 orange
2 large onions, finely chopped
2 to 3 tbs. butter
2 tsp. curry powder

1 tsp. salt
1 can (1 lb.) apricot halves
1 tbs. tomato paste
hot steamed rice
toasted slivered almonds

Cut meat into 1/2 inch strips, discarding fat. Cut orange peel in thin strips. Using a flameproof casserole or Dutch oven, saute onions in 2 tablespoons of butter until glazed and limp. Add curry powder and cook 1 minute. Push onions to the sides of the pan. Add meat and brown on all sides. If necessary, add additional butter. Add salt, apricot halves and juice, tomato paste and orange strips. Cover and bake in a 300° F. oven 2 hours. Stir once or twice to mash the apricots. Serve over hot rice tossed with almonds. Makes 6 servings.

Note: Use a vegetable peeler to peel the orange in long strips. Then use a French knife to cut strips into 1/8 inch pieces.

ALSATIAN BAECKAOFFA

This is a beloved provincial stew from the picturesque wine villages of Alsace. It utilizes the fruity dry white wines of the region to flavor layered meats and potatoes.

1 lb. boneless pork loin
1 lb. boneless calf or veal
3 cloves garlic, minced
1 bay leaf
1 tsp. salt
freshly ground pepper
1/4 tsp. thyme

1/4 cup parsley
2 shallots or green onions, chopped
2 cups Pinot Blanc or Riesling wine
4 large potatoes
2 medium onions
2 tbs. butter
grated Romano or Parmesan cheese

Cut both pieces of meat into 1 inch cubes. Place in a bowl. Add garlic, bay leaf, salt, pepper, thyme, parsley, shallots, and wine. Cover and refrigerate overnight. Peel and thinly slice potatoes and onions. Butter a 2-1/2-quart baking dish. Alternate layers of potatoes, sliced onions and marinated meats. Pour wine marinade over layers. Dot with butter. Cover and bake in a 325° F. oven 2 hours or until meat is tender. Pass cheese to sprinkle over each serving. Makes 6 servings.

CASSOULET

This bourgeoise French bean stew becomes even more succulent when reheated.

1-1/2 cups Great Northern beans
1 lb. boneless pork
1 lb. boneless lamb
3 slices bacon, diced
2 medium onions, chopped
2 cups dry red wine
1 cup beef stock

3 tbs. brandy or Cognac
4 cloves garlic, minced
2 tbs. tomato paste
1-1/2 tsp. salt
1/2 tsp. crumbled dried thyme
1 lb. Italian garlic sausages
chopped parsley

Cover beans with water. Heat and boil 2 minutes. Cover and set aside 1 hour. Drain. Cut pork and lamb in pieces. Saute bacon and onion until glazed. Push to sides of pan. Brown pork and lamb. Combine all remaining ingredients except sausages and parsley in large greased casserole. Cover and bake in 350° F. oven 2 hours. Cover sausages with water and bring to boil. Set aside for 20 minutes. Drain sausages and slice on the diagonal. Arrange on top of casserole. Continue baking 20 to 30 minutes. Sprinkle with parsley. Makes 8 servings.

BEEF BOURGIGNONNE

The **Express** menu of *Les Trois Faisans* in Dijon features this aromatic stew. The surprise fillip is toasted garlic bread splashed with Vermouth.

2 lbs. stewing beef
2 slices bacon, diced
1 small onion, chopped
2 tsp. sugar
2 tsp. red wine vinegar
1 cup dry red wine
1/2 cup beef stock
1 tsp. salt
1 tbs. tomato paste

2 cloves garlic, minced
1/2 tsp. thyme
2 tbs. cornstarch
2 tbs. brandy or Cognac
3 tbs. butter
1 can (15 oz.) small whole onions, drained
6 slices garlic-buttered French bread
2 tbs. dry Vermouth

Cut stew beef into 1-1/2 inch pieces. Using a large Dutch oven, saute bacon until crisp. Remove from pan and set aside. Saute onion in drippings until golden. Push to side of pan. Add meat and saute until lightly browned. Add sugar and vinegar. Cook until meat is well glazed. Stir in wine, stock, salt, tomato paste, garlic, thyme and reserved bacon. Cover and bake in a 300° F. oven 2 hours, or until meat is tender. Remove from oven and place pot over medium heat. Blend cornstarch and brandy. Stir into stew and simmer until thickened. Saute whole onions in remaining butter until lightly browned. Add to stew. Heat French bread in a 400° F. oven until hot through and crispy, about 10 minutes. Sprinkle each bread slice with a few drops of Vermouth. Serve stew in individual bowls. Garnish with slices of hot garlic bread. Makes 6 servings.

OVEN TIME
2-1/2 TO 4 HOURS

BEEF AND ONIONS VASSILI

If you were to peek into the pots of a Greek taverna kitchen, this aromatic stew with its sweet caramelized onions would be certain to entice you. This party size version designed for a dozen is easily divided for a smaller group.

4 lbs. beef rump roast
2 lbs. small whole onions
1/4 cup butter
1-1/2 cups dry red wine
1/3 cup red wine vinegar
1/3 cup tomato paste
2 tbs. brown sugar
3 tsp. salt
6 cloves garlic
2 tsp. mixed pickling spice
2 sticks cinnamon

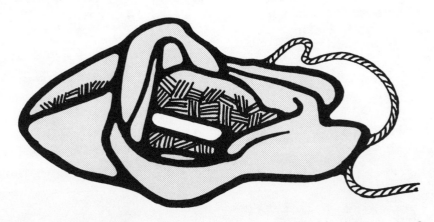

Cut roast into 1-1/2 inch cubes. Using a large frying pan, slowly saute onions in 3

tablespoons butter until barely golden, about 20 minutes. Melt remaining butter in a Dutch oven or flame-proof casserole. Brown meat cubes well. Add onions, wine, vinegar, tomato paste, brown sugar, salt and garlic. Tie pickling spice and cinnamon in a small piece of cheesecloth and add to stew. Cover and bake in a 300° F. oven 2-1/2 hours or until meat is tender. Sprinkle with minced parsley. Makes 12 servings. Serve with Steamed Rice with Pine Nuts.

Steamed Rice with Pine Nuts—Steam 2 cups long-grain white rice in 4-1/2 cups water to which 2 teaspoons salt has been added, until tender. Melt and lightly brown 1/2 cup butter. Pour over rice and sprinkle with 1/3 cup pine nuts. Makes 12 servings.

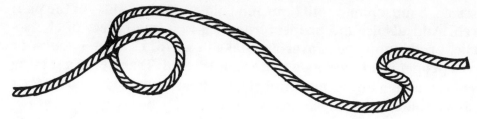

KARELIAN RAGOUT

This inviting Finnish casserole is served with colorful toppings.

1 lb. stewing beef	1 bay leaf
1 lb. stewing pork	2 cloves garlic, minced
4 tbs. butter	1 cup beef broth
3 large onions, sliced	1/2 cup dry white wine
12 whole allspice	1 sweet red pepper, diced
6 whole peppercorns	1/4 lb. mushrooms, sliced
1-1/2 tsp. salt	

Cut beef and pork into 1-1/4 inch pieces. Melt 2 tablespoons butter in a large Dutch oven or flame-proof casserole. Saute onions until limp and golden. Push to sides of the pan. Add meat and brown well. Add allspice and peppercorns, tied in a small piece of cheese-cloth, salt, bay leaf, garlic, broth and wine. Cover and bake in a 275° F. oven 4 hours, or until fork tender. Saute red pepper in 1 tablespoon butter until glazed. Transfer to a serving bowl. Saute mushrooms in remaining butter just until glazed. Place in a serving bowl. Pass toppings to spoon over stew. Makes 6 servings.

LAMB CURRY KRALIK

This entree is easily doubled or tripled for a crowd. Serve with crunchy, Indian pappadums, rice pilaff, raw spinach salad and melon wedges or fresh pineapple.

1 tbs. butter
2 lbs. lean stewing lamb, cubed
1 medium onion, finely chopped
1 tart green apple, peeled and diced
2 tbs. curry powder
salt and pepper to taste
2 cups chicken broth

1/4 cup dry Vermouth
condiments: salted cashews
Major Grey's chutney
toasted coconut
chopped green onions
crumbled crisp bacon

Melt butter in a Dutch oven or flameproof casserole. Brown meat on all sides. Push to the sides of pan. Add onion, apple and curry powder. Cook until onions and apple are transparent. Season with salt and pepper. Add chicken stock and Vermouth. Cover and bake in 300° F. oven 2-1/2 to 3 hours, or until meat is very tender. If desired, cook over high heat to reduce juices slightly. Serve with condiments. Makes 6 servings.

CHOUCROUTE GARNI

This Alsatian country-style dish makes a superb one-dish party meal. Offer at least 3 or 4 kinds of sausages for a unique tasting experience. Traditional accompaniments are Dijon-style mustard, dill pickles and crusty sour dough French bread.

2 slices bacon
2 large onions, chopped
4 pork chops
2 large jars sauerkraut (about 4 lbs.)
2 tart cooking apples
3 cloves garlic, minced
10 peppercorns
2 cups dry white wine
2 lbs. assorted sausages; bratwurst, knackwurst, Polish kielbasa,
   veal frankfurters, cocktail frankfurters,
   Italian garlic sausage, or French wine sausage

In a large frying pan cook bacon until crisp. Add onions and saute until limp. **Push**

Dill Pickles, Dijon-style Mustard, Boiled Potatoes

aside. Add pork chops and brown on both sides. Place sauerkraut in a colander and rinse thoroughly under cold running water. Drain well. Peel, core and slice apples. Combine sauerkraut, apples, pork chops and onions, garlic, peppercorns and wine in a large casserole. Cover and bake in a 300° F. oven 2-1/2 hours. Parboil sausages if necessary. Add to choucroute and continue baking until sausages are thoroughly heated, about 15 minutes longer. Makes 8 servings.

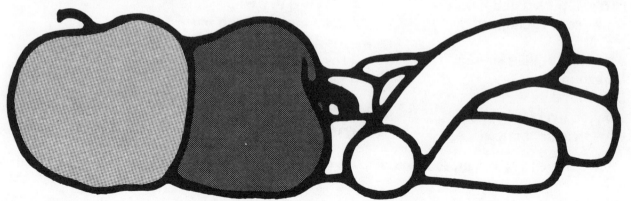

83

BOLOGNESE MEAT SAUCE

This succulent herb-scented pasta sauce achieves distinction through its long slow cooking. Make in quantity, as it is a versatile key to countless dishes. Spoon it over spaghetti or tagliariana, incorporate it in lasagne or manicotti or blend with ricotta cheese and stack between crepes for a festive pie.

2 onions, finely chopped
2 carrots, peeled and grated
2 stalks celery, chopped
olive oil
3/4 lb. mild Italian sausage
1 lb. ground beef
1 lb. ground veal
3 chicken livers, chopped
3 cloves garlic, minced

1 can (8 ozs.) tomato sauce
1-1/4 cups dry white wine
2 tbs. chopped fresh basil
    or 2 tsp. dried basil
2 tbs. chopped parsley
3 beef bouillon cubes
salt and pepper
1/3 cup heavy cream
1/3 cup mushrooms, chopped

In a large Dutch oven, saute onions, carrots and celery in 2 tablespoons oil until glazed.

Remove casings from sausage. Add to vegetables along with beef, veal and chopped livers. Saute until meats begin to brown. Crumble with a fork. Add garlic, tomato sauce, wine, basil, parsley and bouillon cubes. Season with salt and pepper. Cover and bake in a 275° F. oven 3 hours. Stir occasionally. Skim off fat. Add cream and simmer over low heat until desired consistency. Saute mushrooms in 2 tablespoons olive oil. Add to sauce. Makes enough sauce for about 1-1/2 pounds spaghetti or 8 to 10 servings.

GREEK MEAT SAUCE

This lively spiced meat sauce is the basis for numerous Aegean dishes, such as moussaka, pastitsio, or served over Italian green beans and topped with sliced avocado or baked with garden vegetables. Make in quantity and freeze.

4 medium onions
1/4 cup butter
4 lbs. lean ground beef
4 cloves garlic, minced
2 tsp. whole mixed pickling spices
1 stick cinnamon

4 cans (6 oz. ea.) tomato paste
4 tsp. salt
freshly ground pepper
1/4 cup red wine vinegar
1 cup water

Finely chop onions. Melt half the butter in a large Dutch oven. Saute onions until golden brown. Remove from pan and set aside. Brown meat in remaining butter, stirring to make it crumbly. Return onions to pan. Add garlic, pickling spices tied in a small piece of cheesecloth, cinnamon stick, tomato paste, salt, pepper, vinegar and water. Cover and bake in a 275° F. oven 3 to 4 hours. Stir occasionally. Makes about 3 quarts.

INDEX